Schopenhauer's Porcupine

Alice Brière-Haquet

Woodcut illustrations by Olivier Philipponneau

INTRODUCTION

Arthur Schopenhauer (1788–1860) was a German philosopher and a proponent of a rather pessimistic philosophy. Schopenhauer was influenced by Buddhist thought and, like Buddhism, he sought to find solutions to the suffering of life. Deeply cynical of love and the want for children, he believed humans are not so different from non-human animals – just far more unhappy, because of our self-awareness. He used several animals to illustrate his arguments, including the porcupines featured here. His writings influenced later existential philosophy and Freudian psychology, and his most notable work is *The World as Will and Representation* (1819).

The porcupine dilemma is a parable that illustrates the challenges of human intimacy. A group of porcupines huddle together to keep warm on a cold day, but they must separate as they hurt one another with their spines. They all want a close relationship, but the risk of pain draws them away.

Schopenhauer believed that human intimacy unavoidably breeds annoyance and frustration, which in turn encourages superficial relationships.

In the cold winter weather,
the porcupines huddle together.

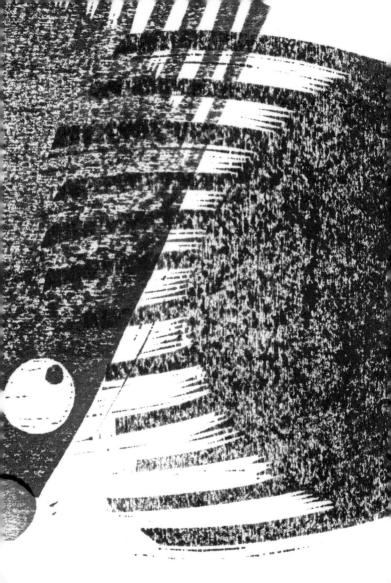

So they go their separate
ways and get cold.

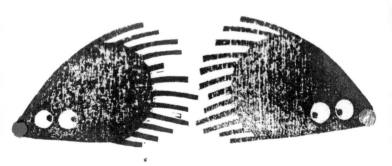

So they huddle together again to warm up, and then separate again.

Huddle together,
hurt each other,
separate, get cold.

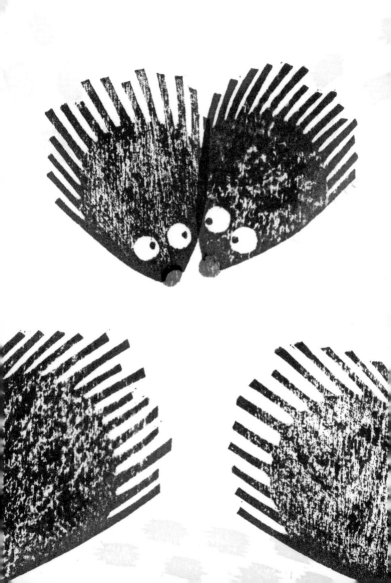

They spend the
season living like
an accordion.

People are the same,
and not just in winter.

When bored, they look for company
but everything about other
people's lives get on their nerves:

their good qualities as much as
their bad qualities, their achievements
just as much as their wounds.

So they back away,
then return again.

But porcupines have the solution: contact in moderation and good manners.

These good manners
allow us to love each other
without being hurt.